W9-AFS-726

HOW TO HELP

A GUIDE TO
**Giving
Back**

VOLUNTEERING
IN YOUR
SCHOOL

Claire O'Neal

Mitchell Lane
PUBLISHERS

P.O. Box 196
Hockessin, DE 19707
www.mitchelllane.com

PUBLISHERS

HOW TO HELP

A GUIDE TO
Giving
Back

Ways to Help After a Natural Disaster
Ways to Help Children With Disabilities
Ways to Help Chronically Ill Children
Ways to Help Disadvantaged Youth
Ways to Help in Your Community
Ways to Help the Elderly
Volunteering in Your School
Celebrities Giving Back

Library of Congress
Cataloging-in-Publication Data

O'Neal, Claire.
 Volunteering in your school / by Claire
O'Neal.
    p. cm. — (How to help : a guide to giving
back)
 Includes bibliographical references and
index.
 ISBN 978-1-58415-920-9 (library bound)
 1. Service learning—Juvenile literature.
 2. Voluntarism—Juvenile literature. I. Title.
 LC220.5.O54 2011
 361.3'7—dc22
                                    2010011982

Printing   1   2   3   4   5   6   7   8   9

PLB

CONTENTS

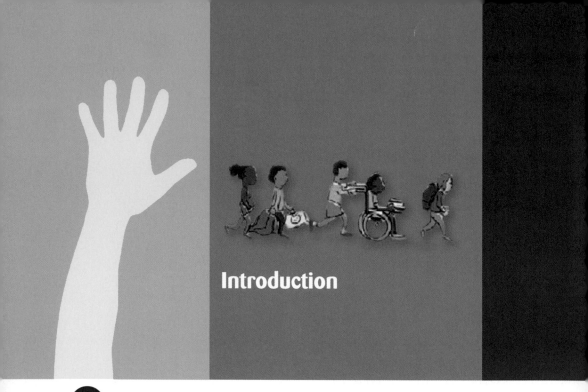

Introduction

On average, U.S. children spend over 1,000 hours in school each year. School is almost like a second home, one that teaches students how to learn and how to live. No one knows a school better than its students. You know your school isn't perfect. Have you ever wondered what you could do to make it better?

Young people just like you have great ideas on how to improve their schools, combined with the passion and energy to get things done. Schools are beginning to recognize a win-win volunteer situation—students represent an army of excited and free labor, while volunteer experiences teach skills and life lessons in a way that can't be taught in a classroom. Studies show that kids who volunteer are more likely to stay in school, get better grades, and go to college.[1] Students who volunteer gain self-confidence. When they volunteer at school, they motivate teachers and other students to do their best, because they show that education really matters. In 2008, 68 percent of school principals in the United States said that their school supports student community service.[2] Growing in popularity, too, are service-learning programs, where volunteering is required for graduation.

Some parents or school staff might cling to the more traditional belief that adults should carry the volunteer load. Sure, you might not

1. HandsOn Network. "Reduce the Drop-out Rate by Leveraging the Power of Service in Every School." http://handsonnetwork.org/impact/education
2. Corporation for National and Community Service. "Community Service and Service Learning in America's Schools." 2008.

have a car or much money to donate, but there's still so much that students like you can do to help out. This book is filled with ideas for volunteer projects that you can do for your school. Whether you volunteer for fun or as a school requirement, students and teachers alike will appreciate your efforts.

Consider these tips to make your volunteer experience great:

- Always get permission from your parents before volunteering. You'll need their help getting to and from school after hours, as well as their advice and help.
- Involve your family, friends, and school staff. Some project ideas are just too big to keep to yourself!
- Turn your hobbies into volunteer opportunities. Do you like playing soccer? Ask the gym teacher if you could donate soccer equipment or help with sports units in gym class. If you like hanging out with friends, you'd make a great student guide or peer tutor.
- Give yourself time to adjust to volunteering. Pushing yourself to try something new will help you grow and learn as a person, but don't be surprised if you feel nervous or out of place at first. A good rule of thumb is to stick with any new experience for three sessions. If you like it, great! If not, find another way to volunteer that suits you better.
- Most important, have fun, and feel proud knowing that any volunteer work you do makes your school a better place.

Students can learn about the food, hobbies, and history of the other cultures found in school at a diversity fair.

Chapter 1

Celebrate Diversity in Your School

Hosting an International Cultural Fair lets students showcase the best their culture has to offer.

You've heard the phrase "It's a small world." This is especially true in Carmel, Indiana. At Carmel High School, informational brochures are translated into a dozen different languages—thanks to school staff and the school's International Club—to serve the needs of families who come from around the world to live in this Indianapolis suburb.

Since the law requires that all kids in a community attend, many schools are melting pots where kids of different races, nationalities, and backgrounds meet to learn together. Working and learning with people who are different teaches students to consider other viewpoints and beliefs, making them more thoughtful and tolerant of others. However, families who recently emigrated to the United States can easily feel out of place at school. Their children are expected to excel at subjects in strange languages and to practice unusual customs and traditions.

You can help bring school families together to celebrate the richness of a multicultural community like yours. Host an International or Cultural Fair, where students can showcase the best their culture has to offer. Everyone will learn more about each other, and about the world beyond their country's borders.

Think about it. Discuss your idea with your friends, teachers, and the principal. Figure out what countries might be represented, and how many people to expect.

When and where should you hold the event? Try to think of a time and place that works for most students and parents. For example, West Park Elementary in Newark, Delaware, hosts Multicultural Night on a Thursday evening each January. The cafeteria serves as the meeting place. You might also use your school gym or have displays set up in the hallways. Your principal and the building manager can show you where to find enough tables and chairs to make your event comfortable.

Do it! Post flyers in the hall with event information, and speak during morning announcements. Ask the principal if you can include a note about the cultural fair in the school newsletter. Recruit parent and student volunteers to help spread the word, and to help you on the day of the event.

Encourage students to bring traditional food from their culture, or to put together a special activity (such as origami from Japan). If they have special talents, invite students to put on a short performance from their culture. They could sing traditional songs, tell folktales from different countries, or perform traditional dances, for example.

As the event draws near, nail down the specifics. How many chairs and tables will you need? Will you need special equipment for food? Ask performers if they will need a radio or microphone. A teacher or building manager can help you find these things in advance.

Report for the cultural fair early to set up tables, chairs, and a stage if necessary. During the event, be sure to take pictures for the school newsletter. Ask families to stay after to help clean up and put equipment away, if they can.

If you like planning events that bring the school's families together, you could also host other theme nights:

- *Math or Science Night.* Find several adults, such as your math and science teachers, parents you know who are engineers or scientists, and students from a nearby university—to help you organize activities. Just like a science or children's museum, you can set up stations for calculator games, paper airplane engineering, or building boats in a baby pool, to give a few examples.
- *Family Fun Night.* Plan gym-type games for families, such as basketball, soccer, or toss-across. Set out board games. Bring a karaoke machine! Sell pizza, popcorn, and drinks, and donate the proceeds to the school.
- *Career Night.* Recruit parents, neighbors, and teachers to share experiences and information about their chosen careers.
- *Literacy or Reading Night.* Recruit parents or your local librarian to tell stories to an audience. Set up tables devoted to different popular authors, with one table for students to write their own stories. Bring your magnetic poetry set and let your school create a poem together! Work with your school's PTA leaders to host a book fair at the same time to make money for the school.

Chapter 2

Start a Peer Tutoring Program

Kids who seek tutors are just like you. They need encouragement and support more than anything else.

High school—and college—may seem very far away, but how well you do in school now sets the stage for how you will perform in the future. More than 6,000 high schoolers drop out every day[1]—each year, that's one in every three students just like you.

Kids who are falling behind have the potential to be great learners; most just need a little extra time and help. Working with other students who have already had the same classes or teachers can give struggling students just the perspective they need to get on track.

In peer tutoring, student tutors help other students one on one. Peer tutors don't give out answers; they help their fellow students learn. Becoming a peer tutor can be very rewarding. Your tutees' successes bring pride to you and to them, and teaching them helps you to be a stronger student, too.

Think about it. Find a teacher to be your sponsor, serving as a contact person for interested students. Together,

1. HandsOn Network. "Reduce the Drop-out Rate by Leveraging the Power of Service in Every School." http://handsonnetwork.org/impact/education

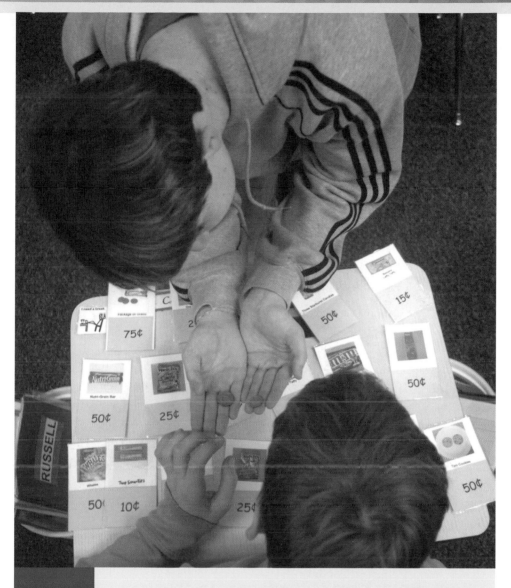

Students in the High Rollers volunteer program at Dixon-Smith Middle School in Stafford, Virginia, serve as buddies to autistic students. Eighth grader Zach Swaney (holding coins) and other High Rollers hang out with the special education class after school or during lunch, reading to the students or playing educational games.

determine a time and place to hold tutoring sessions. It will probably be most convenient for everyone to stay after school together, like a club.

Run your idea by your principal, and ask for permission to hold tutoring sessions in the building after school. In the meantime, approach other teachers with your idea. They can offer names of potential tutors and give you an idea of what subjects will require the most help.

Do it! Advertise! Use flyers and morning announcements to inform students schoolwide about peer tutoring. Recruit kids who want tutoring (called *tutees*), as well as potential tutors, this way. Suggest that interested students leave their information with your sponsor teacher.

Hold a special meeting with peer tutors and your sponsor teacher to match tutors with subjects and tutees. Keep in mind that peer tutoring usually works best with an older tutor and a younger student, especially when the tutor has already had the class or teacher with which the tutee needs help.

Hold your first tutoring session. When you and other tutors meet your first tutees, be polite and patient. Listen to their needs and never judge. Tutees may feel shy, ashamed, or even insulted that they need help. Keep in mind that kids who seek tutors are just like you. They need encouragement and support more than anything else. You might share a story about a time when you needed help in school to put them at ease. It won't be long before you both enjoy learning from each other and growing as students.

If you like helping students one on one, try:

- Becoming a school guide for new students.
- Starting a homework hotline, online chat room, or Facebook group where kids can chat with tutors.
- Operating a student support phone line. Students can call if they need someone to talk to about their problems.

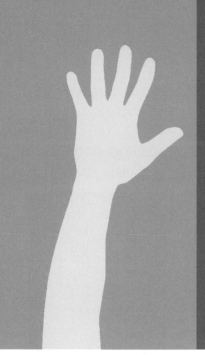

Chapter **3**

Form an After-school Club

Advertise your new club, including its meeting time and place, on flyers in the halls and cafeteria.

Do you have a hobby? Some people collect baseball cards. Others like to sing or dance. Still others like to knit, learn languages, or program computers. Chances are, if it interests you, it will interest other students too. Perhaps you've heard friends from another school talking about how much fun they have in debate club or Spanish club, and wished your school had programs like that. Why not start a school club yourself?

Think about it. What kind of club would you like to start? Poll students with a few choices of activities that interest you, either by asking around or passing out questionnaires. Find out what kind of new club most people would join. As the saying goes, the more the merrier—you'll have more fun, and better luck getting your club going, with more members.

Do it! Find a teacher to sponsor your club, and get permission from the principal, too. Let them know how many kids you think will join the club, how often you might meet, and what you will need from the school (such as meeting rooms). If you know about similar clubs at other schools, come armed with details about how their club operates. The principal can help you refine your ideas and make sure the rooms you need are available.

Advertise your new club, including its meeting time and place, on flyers in the halls and cafeteria. Give out your

An after-school math club is a great way to challenge kids who like math, puzzles, or games, or to offer extra help to students who need it.

name and your sponsor teacher's name as contacts. Keep track of how many kids seem interested.

Host your first meeting. Be on time! Come prepared with a short speech to introduce yourself and what your ideas are for the club. Invite participants to share their ideas, too. Before you end the meeting, come up with an agenda—a list of things to do at your next few meetings.

Hold regular club meetings. Recruit new members through morning announcements, short ads in the school newsletter, and word of mouth. If you are Internet savvy, create a club website or Facebook page. Websites are a great way to help members share news and to provide interested kids with information about the club.

As your club grows, you may want to elect officers to help club members share in the responsibilities. A club president leads the meetings each time. A vice president assists the president, and leads when the president can't make it. The secretary takes brief notes about what goes on during meetings. The treasurer is in charge of club money, which you might need if you wanted to buy pizza one night or to go on a field trip as a club.

Chapter 4

Become a Teacher's Helper

Get your friends involved and make a Classroom Helpers Club out of it.

Think a minute about your teachers. You see them in the classroom—lecturing, asking questions, giving tests. You don't see the hours of hard work they put in before and after school, and even at home. They grade papers and plan lessons weeks in advance. They also meet with students, call parents, and participate in school events. Your teacher has experience juggling all these duties, but he or she could definitely use some help. A study of elementary school teachers showed that they spend, on average, over 3 hours each day beyond school hours to get everything done.[1]

You can lend a hand! Volunteer to be a classroom helper after school. Any teacher would love extra help. In return, classroom helpers enjoy getting to know their teachers better and feeling like an important part of the school.

Think about it. Approach a teacher and let him or her know you want to help. Get your friends involved and make a Classroom Helpers Club out of it. If one helper is good, an army may be better!

1. Smaller, Harry. "Teacher Informal Learning and Teacher Knowledge: Theory, Practice, and Policy." *International Handbook of Educational Policy,* eds. Nina Bascia, Alister Cumming, Amanda Datnow, Kenneth Leithwood, and David Livingstone. Cornwall, U.K.: Springer, 2005, p. 1.

Do it! Agree on a regular time to meet with the teacher. Start by offering your help for an hour a week on a set day and time. If you can't help during your regular time, or if you must be late, give your teacher plenty of notice and offer to make up your volunteer shift. Respect the teacher's time, and he or she will gladly respect yours.

The help the teacher needs will depend on the grade level and subject he or she teaches. Your teacher may ask you to make copies, staple together worksheets or tests, or prepare class materials. All teachers may ask for help tidying up or organizing the classroom. The teacher will train you, showing you how to use the copy machine or where supplies are kept. Listen carefully and take notes if you need to. Ask questions if you don't understand what the teacher has asked of you. Remember that your teacher knows what his or her classroom needs right now. You might have ideas on how to make it better, but save those until you have been a classroom helper for a while.

It will be fun to get to know your teacher outside the classroom, but keep in mind that your teacher might need the time after school to get work done. Once you know how to do the job, suggest that your teacher keep a "project bin" in the classroom for you, where to-do lists and materials can be kept. This way you can dive right in for each volunteer shift, giving the teacher space.

Here are some other ways to help adults one on one:

- Ask your school secretary if you can help out in the office by copying, filing, recording

Help the school librarian tidy up, shelve books, make copies, or set up equipment for library programs.

phone messages, or working on the school newsletter.

- Help the Parent Teacher Association, or PTA. The PTA provides the extras that make schools great. For example, PTA members organize book fairs and school events like family nights and dances. The PTA raises money to sponsor field trips, buy special school equipment, or reward teachers and students. Parents and teachers volunteer their time to accomplish the PTA's many duties. Why not volunteer yours, too? Contact your school's PTA officers and offer your support.

Chapter 5

Reach Out to Kids in Need

Help kids in need start the school year right with a backpack drive.

For many students, back-to-school shopping is a rite of passage. Each September brings new clothes, new shoes, new school supplies. But some kids can't afford back-to-school shopping sprees, even for the most basic supplies.

Alex Lawson, an eleven-year-old from Vero Beach, Florida, had the idea to send donated backpacks filled with supplies to kids in Haiti who were affected by the January 2010 earthquake. Alex asked his school and local places of worship to donate clean backpacks containing a change of clothes, school supplies, and personal care items. Within 48 hours of announcing his idea to his parents, he had collected 400 stuffed backpacks.

Alex's work improved the lives of kids who had lived through a terrible tragedy. But kids all over the world still need help. Even in the United States, the AmeriChild charity estimates that 1 in 5 children live in poverty.[1] You, too, can help kids in need start the school year right with a backpack drive.

1. AmeriChild. "The Cost of Child Poverty in America." http://americhild.org

Think about it. Use the Internet or ask around at community centers, city offices, or your place of worship to find homeless shelters or low-income day care centers in your area that accept school supply donations. Ask them what kinds of supplies their kids need most. Also ask for advice on running a school supply drive—they may have great tips to share. Keep in contact with these organizations so that they are ready for your donations.

Do it! Advertise your cause at school during morning announcements. Get permission from the principal to post detailed flyers in the hall so that students know what kinds of items are needed—new backpacks, pens, pencils, notebooks, folders, and others—and where to put them.

Place a big collection box for donations in a prominent location, such as at the cafeteria entrance. Empty the box each day and keep track of the contents. Keep your school encouraged and informed by reporting each day's total collections during morning announcements.

Approach local stores that sell school supplies, such as Staples or Kmart. Tell them about your cause and ask if they can contribute. Some businesses have donation matching policies—if you collect 15 backpacks at school, would they provide an additional 15?

Recruit students to help organize the supplies. Have a backpack stuffing party after school one day, where volunteers can meet to pack donated bags with pencils, pens, notebooks, and folders. You'll need parents, too, to deliver the stuffed packs.

Report to your school final totals of your backpack drive—how many packs were collected, how many kids and community members participated, and, most important, how many kids you helped.

Your school can help many kids in need. If you like organizing collection drives, here are some other ideas:

The Kits for Kidz program delivers school supply kits to children in need at Stewart Elementary School in Chicago. The charity provides students living in poverty with a year's worth of school supplies, personalized with each student's name and his or her grade level.

- Collect gently used jeans through Teens for Jeans.
- Host a canned food drive for your local food bank.
- Collect toys for Toys for Tots in December.
- Ask students to bring books in good condition to donate to the library or to a struggling local school.

Organize a School Clean-up Day

Advertise School Clean-up Day to students and parents through newsletters and announcements.

You may not look forward to chore day at home—cleaning your room, mowing the lawn, scrubbing the toilet, yuck! But you've probably noticed that keeping your home clean has its advantages. It's less stressful to find your homework, for example, when it's where it belongs.

What works in your room also works in the classroom. Research by Jeffrey Campbell and Alan Bigger confirms what your mom could have told you—kids learn better in clean schools than in dirty ones.[1] Unfortunately, as governments cut school funding, extra cleaning help or repairs are often the first items on the chopping block.

Look around your school with a critical eye. Is it dirty, dingy, or in need of repairs? Are desks scribbled on and scuffed up? Is there trash lying around the halls or on the grounds? If so, you might want to organize a school clean-up day.

1. Campbell, Jeffrey, and Alan Bigger. "Cleanliness and Learning in Higher Education." *Facilities Manager,* July/August 2008, p. 34.

Think about it. Find out who takes care of your school property. This person may have the title of building manager, janitor, or custodian. The person may have assistants, but he or she is still responsible for almost all school repairs and cleaning. Meet with him or her and discuss your ideas. One big clean-up day is great, but perhaps he or she needs regular help, too. Could you and your friends volunteer once a week to be a clean-up crew?

Do it! What equipment will you need for a group of volunteers to clean the school? Will you need volunteers to bring their own trash bags, latex or work gloves, paper towels, and cleaning supplies, or can the school provide those? Ask the building manager, and set a date. Scheduling clean-up day for a Saturday or Sunday afternoon will bring out the most volunteers.

Advertise School Clean-up Day to students and parents through newsletters and announcements. Emphasize how much your school needs their help, and ask people to bring special equipment if necessary. Consider offering free snacks and drinks to attract volunteers. You could ask your parents or the PTA to buy these for you, or consider holding a small fund-raiser (see page 28 for ideas). Post a sign-up sheet so that you know how many people are coming.

Once clean-up day arrives, assign each volunteer a room to clean or a job to accomplish. Some suggestions:

- Are desks wobbly, scratched, or covered with drawings? Ask the custodian to show you what he or she does to fix them. Sandpaper and a fresh coat of paint will make a desk as good as new, helping students to focus on class and not their dirty desk.
- Help with the yard work. Pull weeds and help spread mulch around trees, shrubs, or flowers. During the fall, volunteers can rake leaves; during winter, they can shovel snow from school sidewalks.

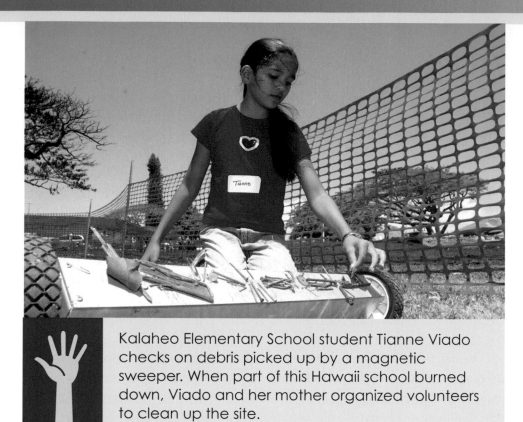

Kalaheo Elementary School student Tianne Viado checks on debris picked up by a magnetic sweeper. When part of this Hawaii school burned down, Viado and her mother organized volunteers to clean up the site.

- Do you like painting? Giving a school room a fresh coat of paint can make it look brand new. If you and your friends are into art, ask your art teacher to help you plan and paint a school mural during clean-up day. What a great way to leave your mark on the school!

Once clean-up day is over, turn your attention to larger repairs that trouble your school. Find a handyman who will donate time to make school repairs. Maybe you know a family member or neighbor who is always working on his house. Could he help at school, too? Consider raising money to buy equipment your school needs. Ask students, parents, and community members to contribute, and your school will reap the benefits for years to come.

Chapter *7*

Green Your School: Recycle

Your school can stand up for the environment by reducing the amount of trash it sends to the landfill.

Did you know that the average American throws away 4.6 pounds of trash every day?[1] Most of that trash goes to landfills, where it gets packed into piles the size of small mountains to sit and rot for years. In the past, landfills have leached chemicals from trash into soil and water, making people sick. Today's landfills obey stricter standards, but they still pollute the air with greenhouse gases emitted from decomposing trash. They also act as enormous, ugly reminders of our wasteful ways.

Your school can stand up for the environment by reducing the amount of trash it sends to the landfill. Much of the waste schools create can be recycled. That aluminum soda can you threw away at lunch? Recycle it, and you'll save enough energy to power a TV for three hours. Want to save seventeen trees? Recycle one ton of paper. If your school doesn't already recycle, you can start a recycling program.

Think about it. What does your school use that can be recycled? Start with paper recycling, and then see if you

1. U.S. Environmental Protection Agency. "Non-Hazardous Waste." http://www.epa.gov/osw/nonhaz/index.htm

can stop all those soda cans and water bottles in the cafeteria from heading to the dump. Computer printer ink cartridges can be recycled, too. Be sure to recycle batteries—from radios, pencil sharpeners, and cell phones—which can leak poisonous chemicals into the environment.

Do it! Find out about recycling programs in your area. Call your city office, local solid waste utility, or recycling company. Ask them for advice on starting a program at your school. Learn what kinds of special bins or Dumpsters they use. Will you need to sort paper, plastic, and cans, or can they be thrown together into one bin? Some programs charge for recycling pickup. Find out what costs are involved, and be sure to ask if your school qualifies for any discounts. If your community does not have recycling pickup yet, get resourceful. Contact parents and teachers: Could they take turns dropping recyclables off at a nearby recycling center?

Work with the building manager to find useful places for recycling bins. Put paper recycling bins in offices, classrooms, and the library; put aluminum and bottle recycling bins in the cafeteria, in the staff room, or near vending machines. Mark each bin clearly so that people can tell the difference between the recycling bin and the trash can. Post flyers above the bins so that students know what goes in them and, more important, what doesn't.

Use announcements and short blurbs in the school newsletter to educate students and teachers on how to recycle at school. Encourage everyone with regular news about school recycling efforts. With the principal's permission, post a chart for everyone to see. You can record what percentage of classrooms are using their recycling bins, or estimate (with the recycling company's help) how much weight you kept out of the landfill. You'll find that the actions of just one school can make a big difference.

In the meantime, look for ways to turn school trash into cash. Can you turn in aluminum soda cans or tabs, steel

Jeffrey Marvel, Hammond Elementary School third grader, sorts his lunch trash. The school has adopted a Waste Free Wednesday program, which makes students aware of the amount of trash they throw away. Students weigh their trash to see which grades recyle the most.

soup cans, or glass or plastic bottles for money? For example, students at Skyline Middle School in Wilmington, Delaware, raised $400 for their school by turning their empty milk bottles over to TerraCycle, a company that uses recyclable materials to make new products.[2] With bottle deposit laws found in eleven U.S. states as of 2010, you can earn a few cents per bottle by bringing glass or plastic bottles to a state redemption center (usually a grocery store). Nationwide, office supply stores such as Staples have printer ink recycling programs that pay several dollars per ink cartridge. Regardless of what programs exist in your area, recycling will benefit your school financially. As less trash goes to the Dumpster, the school will thank you for their lower trash bill.

2. "Skyline Students Raise $400 to Help Beautify School," [Wilmington, Delaware] News Journal, February 7, 2010.

Raise Money for Your School

Get your friends involved to raise money fast.

If there's one thing all schools need, it's money. Between 1987 and 2007, state spending on education rose just 27 percent, while spending on prisons rose 127 percent.[1] Students just like you can raise money to support your school or other worthy causes. These simple, time-tested fund-raising ideas appeal to students, teachers, and parents.

- Ask for money! Approach people one-on-one, or advertise around the school with signs, newsletter articles, and announcements. Explain your cause and, if you can, the equipment or dollar amount needed. Students in the Milwaukee suburb of Wauwatosa raised over $11,000—most in cash, and in less than two months—to support earthquake victims in Haiti.[2] You could easily do the same to buy a new school computer.

1. The Pew Center on the States. "One in 100: Behind Bars in America 2008." February 28, 2008, p. 15. http://www.pewcenteronthestates.org/uploadedFiles/One%20in%20100.pdf
2. Debruin, Isral. "City's Schools Raise More Than $11K to Help Haitians." *Wauwatosa Now*, March 3, 2010. http://www.wauwatosanow.com/news/86265757.html

Molly Clark, 9, left, and her sister, Hannah, 11, work on drawings for a program called ArtStamps that allows children to turn their artwork into postage stamps to raise money for their school.

- Have a schoolwide coin drive. Since 1950, Trick-or-Treat for UNICEF has used this strategy to raise money for kids in need worldwide.[3] Students at American Canyon Middle School in California raised $1,104 in October 2009 through the Trick-or-Treat for UNICEF program, asking for money for poor kids around the world instead of candy on Halloween night.[4] Visit UNICEF online to get collection materials

3. Schoop, Kini. "56 Years Later and Still Unique: Trick-or-Treat for UNICEF." UNICEF Press Centre, 2006. http://www.unicef.org/media/media_36407.html
4. Builder's Club of American Canyon Middle School. http://www3.nvusd.k12. ca.us/education/components/scrapbook/default.php?sectiondetailid=18467& &PHPSESSID=ea3fccbd122e00939861825c09e46b5c

you can use year-round. To raise money for your school, make your own labeled coffee cans or jars and ask to put one in each classroom.

- Is your closet overflowing with clothes, toys, or books you don't need? Have a yard sale and donate the profits to your school. Tell buyers that all proceeds go to your worthy cause. Encourage your friends to join in to raise even more money.

- Start a school store. With your parents' help and permission from the principal, buy school supplies or snacks in bulk at a wholesale club and resell the items for a reasonable price at school.

- Do you earn money for chores around your house, such as mowing the lawn, washing the car, or baby-sitting? Instead of pocketing the cash, consider donating it to the PTA.

- Start a holiday classroom delivery service. For a dollar or two donation, take orders from kids or teachers to deliver small presents to special friends during the school day. For example, you could deliver carnations on Valentine's Day or candy on Halloween. Recruit friends and parents to help you make the promised deliveries.

- Have you seen ads for a fish fry, pancake breakfast, or spaghetti dinner at a local church? These crowd-pleasing meals are inexpensive to prepare. Raise money by hosting a similar event at your school. Ask your cafeteria supervisor for permission to use the school's kitchen, and ask parents and friends to help you gather the ingredients and cook the meals. Charge a good price for some great food, and you'll bring the whole school together to share a meal for a worthy cause.

Chapter **9**

Promote Fitness with a School Race

Hosting a charity race for your school is a great way to encourage fitness in students, teachers, and the community.

Pediatricians recommend that kids get an hour of physical activity every day. Do you? If you're like most kids, you don't. Get Kids in Action reports that less than one-third of U.S. 15-year-olds exercise during the school week, and less than 17 percent stay active on weekends.[1] In the past, every kid could expect to exercise during gym class, but in 2006, fewer than 4 percent of U.S. elementary and fewer than 8 percent of U.S. middle schools offered physical education programs.[2] School officials cut out P.E. to give kids more classroom time and improve testing scores, or because gym teachers and equipment were too expensive. Unfortunately, with one in three American kids categorized as obese,[3] today's school-children need exercise now more than ever.

Isaac Dickson Elementary School in Asheville, North Carolina, came up with a solution that gets kids moving and boosts school budgets at the same time. Each January, kids

1. Get Kids in Action, "Exercise for Kids." http://www.getkidsinaction.org/exercise/
2. Centers for Disease Control. "School Health Policies and Programs Study." 2006. http://www.cdc.gov/HealthyYouth/shpps/2006/factsheets/pdf/FS_Overview_SHPPS2006.pdf
3. Get Kids in Action.

and adults alike participate in the Hot Chocolate 10K Run. They follow different courses: adults run a challenging 10-kilometer (10K) race, while kids 12 and under compete by scrambling up a 1-kilometer hill. Everybody ends the day with a race T-shirt and a cup of hot cocoa. Because participants pay a registration fee typical of such races, the 2010 Hot Chocolate 10K raised over $9,000 for the school.[4]

In 2006, charity races and athletic events raised over $1.5 billion for U.S. nonprofit organizations.[5] Hosting a charity race is a great way to encourage fitness in students, teachers, and the community, all while raising money for your school.

Think about it. How long should your race be? The most common are 5K races. At only a little over 3 miles, most people can walk a 5K; fit adults and kids can run it. Serious racers enjoy 10K races, but at 6.2 miles, they are too long for most kids. If you'd prefer a race for younger kids, consider a 1-mile fun run.

Research other races in your community to determine what race lengths and times of year are popular . . . and then break the mold! You'll attract a following by offering a new kind of race. If a popular 5K race draws crowds in May, schedule yours for February, or hold a 1-mile fun run a few weeks before. Look at registration fees charged by popular races to get an idea of what's reasonable for yours.

Do it! Start planning your race several months in advance, and get help! First, contact a local running store or fitness club. These people know how to organize races—such as what rules and regulations need to be followed at the city level, and where to get equipment to accurately time the race. Next, get parents, friends, and teachers involved. Gather a big team to help you pull off this fun event. Finally, approach local businesses with your race idea. Can they

4. Isaac Dickson Hot Chocolate 10K and Kids Hill Climb. http://www.hotchocolate10k.com/Default.aspx
5. Run Walk Ride Foundation. "RWRF 101." http://runwalkride.com/marketing_101.asp

donate money or supplies, such as tables and chairs or water bottles for runners?

Design your race course with your runner in mind. Have your parents drive you around your school or community. Running trails—paved or not—are ready-made for footraces. If you find a pretty street that just begs for a run, call the city police and ask if they could shut it down for a few hours on the day of the race. Once you finalize your course, call your city offices for details on what the rules are and whom you can ask for help.

Advertise your race—when, where, and how to sign up— at school, but reach a larger audience, too, at local gyms and fitness clubs. Contact your city offices and ask if you can put an ad for your fund-raiser on the town website. Ask the local newspaper if you can post an ad about the race for free or at reduced cost. If you have any experience with the Internet, creating a race website or Facebook page will provide interested runners with the information they need.

Ask the PTA or school office to manage the registration money. Set aside some of the money to buy prizes for participants, like T-shirts with a logo for your school race. Donate the rest to the school. Report how much the race earns in the school newsletter; kids and parents alike will enjoy seeing how their efforts reward the school.

On the day of the race, divide volunteers into teams to man the registration table, hand out runner name tags or numbers, and supervise timing equipment. Make sure to run your own race, and have fun watching people get fit for a great cause!

If you like being healthy and active, try:

- Starting a walking or running club at school.
- Advertising TV Turn-Off Weeks, which take place nationwide in April and September.
- Raising money to buy school gym equipment.

Chapter 10

Plant a School Garden

Schools with vegetable gardens show great improvement in science test scores.

At the Samuel Green Charter School in New Orleans, Louisiana, students spend the whole year thinking about food. Part of their lunch comes from the school garden. Students in every grade spend time preparing the soil, planting, weeding, and harvesting fresh vegetables and herbs from the garden. Then they help cook the veggies in soups, salads, and stir-fries, seeing for themselves how delicious fresh-grown produce can taste.[1]

Just like Samuel Green Charter, schools all over the United States are taking charge, turning their land into a healthy future for students' bodies and minds. Taking care of plants provides students with hands-on lessons in plant and insect biology, as well as planning and responsibility. Schools with vegetable gardens show great improvement in science test scores. Students get to work outside on nice days, getting fresh air and exercise. With a little planning, school garden harvests go straight onto students' lunch trays, making fresh, nutritious, and great-tasting meals. And because most schools'

1. Smith, Natalie. "Food for Thought." *Junior Scholastic,* April 13, 2009.

vegetable gardens are grown largely based on volunteer efforts, they might even make lunch more affordable.

You can help bring a vegetable garden to your school.

Think about it. Talk with your teachers, principal, and the school district's main office about your idea. You'll need their advice—and permission—before you proceed. Get to know your school groundskeeper as well. He or she can help you turn your planting ideas into reality.

A garden rewards your school with food, fun, and learning experiences for years to come, but getting it started can be a lot of work. Get help! Get your parents on board with your idea first. Next, approach your school's PTA, who can command an army of parent volunteers. Expect a lot of excited parent volunteers!

Do it! Once the school gives the garden a green light, contact your local Master Gardener to help you plan. These experienced gardeners volunteer their time to help people with all kinds of gardening questions. Master Gardener contact information by state can be found at the American Horticultural Society website (http://www.ahs.org/master_gardeners/). Together, you can think about which vegetables grow quickly enough to be planted and harvested during the school year. For example, lettuce, radishes, peas, and carrots can be planted early in the spring and harvested before school lets out for summer.

Set two dates—one to build and prepare the garden beds, and another, a week later, for planting. What kinds of materials will you need? Parents at your school can probably lend shovels and gardening gloves. Call your city's main office to find out if they have a green-waste recycling program, where you can get mulch for free.

A school garden cannot be totally free, however. Soil and plants cost money, varying from tens to thousands of dollars,

At Emerson Elementary School in Riverside, California, Green Team students volunteer their lunch recess to tend the school garden. The students also enjoy a nationally recognized program that brings farm-fresh produce to their school lunches.

depending on which plants you want and the size of your garden. You can keep the price low by starting small and working with plants donated from gardener friends, or by planting inexpensive blackberry or raspberry canes instead of vegetables. Ask gardeners in your neighborhood if they have healthy plants they could give to your cause. If you need money, consider the fund-raising ideas on page 28. Some gardens are funded with grants from the government. Ask your school principal for ideas on applying for local, state, or even federal money.

Recruit a team of helpers to dig out and prepare the beds, as well as to buy, transport, and plant the plants. With the groundskeeper's help, choose the sunniest possible spot to plant the new garden. Encourage the whole school to join in for the first planting.

Coordinate student and parent volunteers to help with the weeding, planting, and harvesting. Make a plan with the building manager to water the garden on a near-daily basis. Better yet, find teachers interested in the garden and ask them to incorporate garden duty into their lesson plans. Successful programs like Delaware's Healthy Foods for Healthy Kids have lesson plans already available (http://healthy foodsforhealthykids.giving.officelive.com/default.aspx). Most important, have fun growing your own food and eating it!

If you like digging in the dirt, try:

- Planting a tree at school. You can make it a com-memorative tree to remember your class or a special event.
- Planting a butterfly garden.
- Building a school compost pile. Cafeteria workers can keep food waste out of the landfill and turn it into healthy and earth-friendly fertilizer to use on the school grounds.

National Organizations
Boy Scouts of America
  http://scouting.org
Builders Club—http://slp.kiwanis.org/
  BuildersClub/Homepage.aspx
Do Something
  http://www.dosomething.org
Feeding America
  http://feedingamerica.org
Girl Scouts of America
  http://girlscouts.org
Goodwill Industries, Inc.
  http://www.goodwill.org/
HandsOn Network
  http://vop.handsonnetwork.org/
Idealist Kids and Teens
  http://www.idealist.org/kt/
Kids Care Club—http://www.kidscare.org/
Kits for Kidz—http://www.kitsforkids.org/
Learn and Serve
  http://www.servicelearning.org/
National Youth Leadership Council
  http://www.nylc.org/
Parent Teacher Association (PTA)
  http://www.pta.org/
Planet Protectors Club
  http://www.epa.gov/osw/education/
  kids/planetprotectors/index.htm
Teens for Jeans—http://www.dosomething.
  org/teensforjeans/home
TerraCycle
  http://www.terracycle.net
United We Serve—http://www.serve.gov
Youth Venture—http://www.genv.net/

Alabama
Alabama State Department of Education
50 North Ripley St.
P.O. Box 302101
Montgomery, AL 36104
(334) 242-9700
http://www.alsde.edu/

Reduce Class Size Now
2888 Ponce de Leon Ct.
Gulf Shores, AL 36542
(251) 540-7012
http://www.reduceclasssizenow.org

VOICES for Alabama's Children
P.O. Box 4576
Montgomery, AL 36103
(334) 213-2410
http://www.alavoices.org

Alaska
Alaska Conservation Foundation
441 West Fifth Ave., Ste. 402
Anchorage, AK 99501-2340
(907) 276-1917
http://alaskaconservation.org/

Alaska Department of Education and Early
  Development
801 West 10th St., Ste. 200
P.O. Box 110500
Juneau, AK 99811
(907) 465-2800
http://www.eed.state.ak.us/

Challenge Alaska
P.O. Box 1166
Girdwood, AK 99587
(907) 783-2925
http://www.challengealaska.org/

Sitka Tribe of Alaska
456 Katlian St.
Sitka, AK 99835
(907) 747-3207
http://www.servicelearning.org/program/
  sitka-tribe-alaska

Arizona
Arizona Department of Education
1535 West Jefferson St.
Phoenix, AZ 85007
(602) 542-5393
http://www.ade.state.az.us/

Arizona Homegrown Solutions
3851 E. Thunderbird Rd., #111
Phoenix, AZ 85032
(480) 282-8488
http://azhomegrownsolutions.ning.com/

Hope & A Future
P.O. Box 61172
Phoenix, AZ 85082
(602) 258-5860
http://azhope.com/

Youth Count
3343 N. WIndsong Dr., Ste. 6
Prescott Valley, AZ 86314
(928) 708-0100
http://www.youthcount.org/

Arkansas
Arkansas Advocates for Children and
  Families
1400 West Markham, Ste. 306
Little Rock, AR 72201
(501) 371-9678
http://www.aradvocates.org/

Arkansas Department of Education
4 Capitol Mall
Little Rock, AR 72201
(501) 682-4475
http://www.arkansased.org

California
California Department of Education
1430 N St.
Sacramento, CA 95814
(916) 319-0800
http://www.cde.ca.gov/

Samsung's Recycling Fundraiser for San
   Francisco Public Schools
Various Locations
(415) 920-5076
http://www.samsung.com/us/business/
   semiconductor/corporate_info/
   SSIRecyclingFundraiser.html

Youth Service California
P.O. Box 70764
Oakland, CA 94612-0764
(510) 750-8998
http://www.yscal.org/cm/Home.html

Colorado
Children's Voices
1426 Pearl St., Ste. 402
Boulder, CO 80302
(303) 449-6180
http://www.childrens-voices.org/

Colorado Department of Education
201 East Colfax Ave.
Denver, CO 80203
(303) 866-6600
http://www.cde.state.co.us/

A Place to Call Home
331 Clark Street
Sterling, CO 80751
(970) 580-2041
http://aplace2callhome.tripod.com/
   homeless/

Public Education and Business Coalition
1244 Grant St.
Denver, CO 80203
(303) 861-8661
http://www.pebc.org/

Connecticut
Changing Winds Native American
   Advocacy Center
P.O. Box 801
Fairfield, CT 06824
(203) 256-9720
http://www.changingwinds.org

Connecticut Center for School Change
151 New Park Ave., Ste. 203
Hartford, CT 06106
(860) 586-2340
http://www.ctschoolchange.org/

Connecticut State Department of
   Education
165 Capitol Ave.
Hartford, CT 06106
(860) 713-6543
http://www.sde.ct.gov/

Delaware
Delaware Department of Education
401 Federal St.
Dover, DE 19901
(302) 735-4000
http://www.doe.k12.de.us/

Healthy Foods for Healthy Kids
P.O. Box 847
Hockessin, DE 19707
(302) 235-2692
http://healthyfoodsforhealthykids.giving.
   officelive.com/

Read Aloud Delaware
100 W. 10th St., Ste. 309
P.O. Box 25249
Wilmington, DE 19899
(302) 656-5256
http://www.readalouddelaware.org

District of Columbia
D.C. Public Schools
1200 First St., NE
Washington, DC 20002
(202) 442-5885
http://dcps.dc.gov/portal/site/DCPS/

District of Columbia Public Charter School
   Board
3333 14th St., NW, Ste. 210
Washington, DC 20010
(202) 328-2660
http://www.dcpubliccharter.com/

Greater D.C. Cares
1725 I St. NW, Ste. 200
Washington, DC 20006
(202) 777-4452
http://www.greaterdccares.org/

Florida
Coalition for the Homeless of Central
   Florida
639 West Central Blvd.
Orlando, FL 32801
(407) 426-1250
http://www.centralfloridahomeless.org/
   about_contact.html

Florida Department of Education
Turlington Building, Ste. 1514
325 West Gaines St.
Tallahassee, FL 32399
(850) 245-0505
http://www.fldoe.org/

Florida Education Foundation
325 West Gaines St., Room 1524
Tallahassee, FL 32399-0400
(850) 245-9671
http://www.floridaeducationfoundation.
    org/

Georgia
Georgia Department of Education
2054 Twin Towers East
205 Jesse Hill Jr. Dr. SE
Atlanta, GA 30334
(404) 656-2800
http://www.doe.k12.ga.us/

The Loop It Up Savannah Project
West Broad Street YMCA
1110 May St.
Savannah, GA 31415
(912) 233-1951
http://www.loopitupsavannah.blogspot.
    com/

Hawaii
Christmas Wish Program, Inc./Project
    Hawai'i
P.O. Box 1844
Keaau, HI 96749
(808) 982-8128
http://www.HelptheHomelessKeiki.org

Hawaii Public Schools
1390 Miller St.
Honolulu, HI 96813
(808) 586-3230
http://doe.k12.hi.us/

KAUPA—Kalihi Ahupua'a Ulu Pono Ahahui
P.O. Box 17673
Honolulu, HI 96817
(808) 853-2218
http://www.kaupa4kalihi.org/

Idaho
Coalition of Idaho Charter School Families
P.O. Box 6236
Boise, ID 83707
(877) 792-5900
http://www.idchartercoalition.org/

Idaho State Department of Education
650 West State Street
Boise, ID 83720
(800) 432-4601
http://www.sde.idaho.gov/

Illinois
America's Second Harvest
35 E. Wacker Dr., #2000
Chicago, IL 60601
http://feedingamerica.org/

Illinois State Board of Education
100 N. 1st St.
Springfield, IL 62777
(866) 262-6663
http://www.isbe.state.il.us/

Springfield Public Schools Volunteer
    Opportunities
1900 West Monroe
Springfield, IL 62704
(217) 525-3257
http://www.springfield.k12.il.us/volunteer/

Indiana
Indiana Department of Education
151 West Ohio St.
Indianapolis, IN 46204
(317) 232-6610
http://www.doe.in.gov/

School on Wheels
5420 North College Ave., Ste. 101
Indianapolis, IN 46220
(317) 202-9100
http://www.schoolonwheels.org/

Second Helpings Community Kitchen and
    Food Pantry
The Eugene and Marilyn Glick Center
1121 Southeastern Ave.
Indianapolis, IN 46202
(317) 632-2664
http://www.secondhelpings.org/

Iowa
Care Bags Foundation
c/o Anne Wignall
2713 N. 4th Ave. E.
Newton, IA 50208
http://www.carebags4kids.org/

Iowa Department of Education
400 E 14th St.
Des Moines, IA 50319
(515) 281-5294
http://www.iowa.gov/educate/

Urban Education Network of Iowa
Julio Almanza, Chair
1606 Brady St.
Davenport, IA 52803
almanzaj@mail.davenport.k12.ia.us
http://www.uen-ia.org/contact.htm

Kansas

Communities in Schools of KCK/Wyandotte
  County
4601 State Ave., Ste. 38
Kansas City, KS 66102
(913) 627-4382
https://www.myctb.org/wst/CISKCK/
  default.aspx

Greenbush—Southeast Kansas Education
  Service Center
P.O. Box 189
947 W. 47 Highway
Girard, KS 66743
(620) 724-6281
http://www.greenbush.org/

Kansas State Department of Education
120 SE 10th Ave.
Topeka, KS 66612
(785) 296-3201
http://www.ksde.org/

Kentucky

International Book Project
1440 Delaware Ave.
Lexington, KY 40505
(859) 254-6771
http://www.internationalbookproject.org/

Kentucky Department of Education
500 Mero St.
Frankfort, KY 40601
(502) 564-4770
http://www.education.ky.gov/KDE/

National Center for Family Literacy
325 West Main St., Ste. 300
Louisville, KY 40202
(502) 584-1133
http://www.famlit.org/

Louisiana

Beacon of Hope Resource Center
145 Robert E Lee Blvd., Ste. 200
New Orleans, LA 70124
(504) 309-5120
http://www.lakewoodbeacon.org

HandsOn New Orleans
1050 S. Jefferson Davis Parkway,
  Suites 204 and 212
New Orleans, LA 70125
(504) 483-7041
http://www.handsonneworleans.org

Louisiana Department of Education
1201 North 3rd St.
Baton Rouge, LA 70804
(877) 453-2721
http://www.louisianaschools.net/

Maine

Junior Achievement of Maine
82 Elm St.
Portland, ME 04101
(207) 347-4333
http://maine.ja.org/

KIDS Consortium
223 Main St.
Auburn, ME 04210
(207) 784-0956
http://www.kidsconsortium.org/

Maine Department of Education
23 State House Station
Augusta, ME 04333
(207) 624-6600
http://www.maine.gov/education/

Maryland

Baltimore Algebra Project
2526 North Charles St.
Baltimore, MD 21218-4601
(410) 338-0679; (410) 243-4969
http://www.baltimore-algebra-project.org/

Maryland Business Roundtable for
  Education
5520 Research Park Dr., Ste. 150
Baltimore, MD 21228
(410) 788-0333
http://www.mbrt.org/Default.asp

Maryland State Department of Education
200 W. Baltimore St.
Baltimore, MD 21201
(410) 685-7971
http://www.marylandpublicschools.org/
  msde

Massachusetts

United Way Youth Venture, North Central
  Massachusetts
285 John Fitch Hwy., Ste. 1
Fitchburg, MA 01420
(978) 345-1577
http://www.uwncm.org/

Massachusetts Department of Elementary
  and Secondary Education
75 Pleasant St.
Malden, MA 02148
(781) 338-3000
http://www.doe.mass.edu/

Worcester County Food Bank
474 Boston Turnpike Rd.
Shrewsbury, MA 01545
(508) 842-3663
http://foodbank.org/

Michigan
Lansing Jaycees
P.O. Box 16150
Lansing, MI 48901
http://www.lansingjaycees.org

Michigan Department of Education
608 W. Allegan St.
P.O. Box 30008
Lansing, MI 48909
(517) 373-3324
http://www.michigan.gov/mde

Minnesota
Minnesota Department of Education
1500 Highway 36 West
Roseville, MN 55113
(651) 582-8200
http://education.state.mn.us/mde/index.
   html

St. Paul Public Schools Foundation
55 5th St. East
St. Paul, MN 55101
(651) 325-4254
http://www.sppsfoundation.org

Student Pledge Against Gun Violence
112 Nevada St.
Northfield, MN 55057
(507) 645-5378
http://www.pledge.org

Mississippi
Hope CDA
425 Division
Biloxi, MS 39530
(228) 918-0229
http://www.hopecda.org/

Love's Kitchen
801 18th Ave.
Meridian, MS 39301
(601) 693-1409
http://www.loveskitchenmeridian.com/

Mississippi Department of Education
359 North West St.
Jackson, MS 39201
(601) 359-3513
http://www.mde.k12.ms.us/

Missouri
Lutheran Family and Children's Services of
   Missouri
401 West Blvd. North
Columbia, MO 65203
(573) 815-9955
http://www.lfcsmo.org/volunteer/

Missouri Department of Elementary and
   Secondary Education
205 Jefferson St.
P.O. Box 480
Jefferson City, MO 65102
(573) 751-4212
http://dese.mo.gov/

Project Appleseed
520 Melville Ave.
St. Louis, MO 63130
(314) 292-9760
http://www.projectappleseed.org/

St. Louis Public Schools Volunteer Services
801 N. 11th St.
St. Louis, MO, 63101
(314) 231-3720
http://www.slps.org/19621084161712707/
   site/default.asp

Montana
Montana Food Bank Network
5625 Expressway
Missoula, MT 59808
(406) 721-3825
http://www.mfbn.org/

Montana Office of Public Instruction
P.O. Box 202501
Helena, MT 59620
(406) 444-3095
http://opi.mt.gov/

Nebraska
National Arbor Day Foundation
100 Arbor Ave.
Nebraska City, NE 68410
(888) 448-7337
http://www.arborday.org

Nebraska Department of Education
301 Centennial Mall South
Lincoln, NE 68509
(402) 471-2295
http://www.nde.state.ne.us/

Rural Schools—Center for Rural Affairs
145 Main St., P.O. Box 136
Lyons, NE 68038
(402) 687-2100
http://www.cfra.org/resources/rural_schools

Nevada
ESL In-Home Program of Northern Nevada
702 Sean Dr.
Carson City, NV 89701
(775) 888-2021
http://www.eslinhome.org/

Nevada Department of Education
700 E. Fifth St.
Carson City, NV 89701
(775) 687-9200
http://www.doe.nv.gov/

New Hampshire
Lebanon Recreation and Parks
51 North Park St.
Lebanon, NH 03766
(603) 448-5121
http://recreation.lebnh.net/

Middle New Hampshire Arts and
    Entertainment Center
316 Central St.
Franklin, NH 03235
(603) 934-1901
http://www.themiddlenh.org

New Hampshire Department of Education
101 Pleasant St.
Concord, NH 03301
(603) 271-3494
http://www.education.nh.gov/

New Jersey
Blossom International
P.O. Box 421
Manasquan, NJ 08736
(732) 722 7240
http://blossominternational.org/index/

The LEAGUE National Office
35 James St.
Newark, NJ 07102-2016
(973) 643-6373
http://leagueworldwide.org/

New Jersey Department of Education
P.O. Box 500
Trenton, NJ 08625-0500
(609) 292-4469
http://www.state.nj.us/education

New Mexico
New Mexico Public Education Department
Jerry Apodaca Education Building
300 Don Gaspar
Santa Fe, NM 87501
(505) 827-5800
http://www.ped.state.nm.us/

New York
Children for Children
6 East 43rd St., 25th Floor
New York, NY 10017
(212) 850-4170
http://www.childrenforchildren.org/

Kids Can Make a Difference
140 East 72nd St. #14B
New York, NY 10021
(212) 861-0911
http://www.kidscanmakeadifference.org

New York State Department of Education
89 Washington Ave.
Albany, NY 12234
(518) 474-3852
http://www.nysed.gov/

North Carolina
North Carolina Public Schools
301 N. Wilmington St.
Raleigh, NC 27601
(919) 807-3300
http://www.ncpublicschools.org/

Volunteer in Your Community, Inc.
5710-K High Point Rd., Ste. 221
Greensboro, NC 27407
(336) 669-7667
http://www.viyc.org

North Dakota
Junior Achievement of Bismarck-Mandan
1640 Burnt Boat Dr.
Bismarck, ND 58502
(701) 223-5660
http://www.bismanja.org/

North Dakota Department of Public
    Instruction
600 E. Boulevard Ave., Dept. 201
Bismarck, ND 58505-0440
(701) 328-2260
http://www.dpi.state.nd.us/

Ohio
Grandma's Gifts
P.O. Box 2
Powell, OH 43065
(614) 388-9007
http://grandmasgifts.org/

Hunger Network of Greater Cleveland
614 West Superior Ave.
Cleveland, OH 44113
(216) 619-8155
http://www.hungernetwork.org

Ohio Department of Education
25 South Front St.
Columbus, Ohio 43215
(877) 644-6338
http://www.ode.state.oh.us

Oklahoma
Carrie Garth Wells Institute Inc.
10703 NE 5th St.
Midwest City, OK 73110
(405) 259-9697
http://www.cgwellsinstitute.org

Feed the Children
P.O. Box 36
Oklahoma City, OK 73101
(405) 942-0228
http://www.feedthechildren.org

Oklahoma State Department of Education
2500 N. Lincoln Blvd.
Oklahoma City, OK 73105
(405) 521-3301
http://sde.state.ok.us/

Oregon
Oregon City School District—Volunteers
1417 12th St.
Oregon City, OR 97045
(503) 785-8000
http://www.orecity.k12.or.us/support/
    volunteer

Oregon Department of Education
255 Capitol St. NE
Salem, OR 97310
(503) 947-5600
http://www.ode.state.or.us/

River Network
520 SW Sixth Ave., Ste. 1130
Portland, OR 97204
(503) 241-3506
http://www.rivernetwork.org

Pennsylvania
Pennsylvania Department of Education
333 Market St.
Harrisburg, PA 17126-0333
(717) 783-6788
http://www.education.state.pa.us

Pittsburgh Cares
239 Fourth Ave., Ste. 1007
Pittsburgh, PA 15222
(412) 471-2114
http://www.pittsburghcares.org/

Rhode Island
Childreach
155 Plan Way
Warwick, RI 02886
(800) 556-7918
http://www.childreach.org

Rhode Island Department of Elementary
    and Secondary Education
255 Westminster St.
Providence, RI 02903
(401) 222-4600
http://www.ride.ri.gov/

South Carolina
Communities in Schools
1090 E. Montague Ave.
North Charleston, SC 29405
(843) 740-6793
http://communitiesinschools.org/

South Carolina Department of Education
1429 Senate St.
Columbia, SC 29201
(803) 734-8500
http://ed.sc.gov/

South Dakota
South Dakota Department of Education
700 Governors Dr.
Pierre, SD 57501
(605) 773-3134
http://doe.sd.gov/

South Dakota State University Service-
    Learning Initiative
823 Medary Ave.
Brookings, SD 57007
(605) 697-5015
http://sdsuservice-learning.blogspot.com

Tennessee
Kids for a Clean Environment
P.O. Box 158254
Nashville, TN
(800) 952-3223
http://www.kidsface.org

Tennessee Department of Education
710 James Robertson Parkway
Nashville, TN 37243
(615) 741-2731
http://www.state.tn.us/education/

Texas
Austin Voices for Education and Youth
3710 Cedar St., Ste. 229, Box 21
Austin, TX 78705
(512) 450-1880
http://www.austinvoices.org/

Challenge Air for Kids & Friends
7363 Cedar Springs Rd.
Dallas, TX 75235
(214) 351-3353
http://www.challengeair.com/

The Military Child Education Coalition
909 Mountain Lion Circle
P. O. Box 2519
Harker Heights, TX 76548
(254) 953-1923
http://www.militarychild.org

Texas Education Agency
1701 N. Congress Ave.
Austin, TX 78701
(512) 463-9734
http://www.tea.state.tx.us/

Utah
Literacy Resources, Inc.
1524 E 1110 N
Orem, UT 84097
(801) 420-3675
http://www.literacyresources.org/

Utah State Office of Education
250 Easl 500 South
Salt Lake City, UT 84114
(801) 538-7500
http://www.schools.utah.gov

Vermont
National Gardening Association
1100 Dorset St.
South Burlington, VT 05403
(800) 538-7476
http://www.kidsgardening.com

Vermont Department of Education
120 State St.
Montpelier, VT 05620
(802) 828-3135
http://education.vermont.gov/

Virginia
Capital Region Earth Force
P.O. Box 2447
Alexandria, VA 22301
(703) 838-9074
http://earthforce.org/section/offices/
    capitalregion

Communities in Schools
2345 Crystal Dr., Ste. 801
Alexandria, VA 22202
(703) 519-8999
http://www.cisnet.org

Virginia Department of Education
P.O. Box 2120
Richmond, VA 23218
(804) 225-2023
http://www.doe.virginia.gov/

Washington
Experience Food Project
Chef Tom French, Director
cheftom@experiencefoodproject.org
(360) 298-4051
http://www.experiencefoodproject.org/

State of Washington Office of the
    Superintendent of Public Instruction
Old Capitol Building
P.O. Box 47200
Olympia, WA 98504
(360) 725-6000
http://www.k12.wa.us/

West Virginia
Direct Action Welfare Group, Inc.
1605 Washington St. W
Charleston, WV 25312
(304) 720-0260
http://www.wvdawg.org

West Virginia Department of Education
1900 Kanawha Blvd. East
Charleston, WV 25305
(304) 558-2681
http://wvde.state.wv.us/

Wisconsin
Waukesha County Backpack Coalition
500 Riverview
Waukesha, WI 53188
(262) 547-7367
http://www.backpackcoalilion.org

Wisconsin Department of Public Instruction
125 S. Webster St
Madison, WI 53707
(800) 441-4563
http://dpi.wi.gov/

Wyoming
Wyoming Afterschool Alliance
626 Washington St.
Lander, WY 82520
(307) 335- 9922
http://www.wyafterschoolalliance.org/

Wyoming Department of Education
2300 Capitol Ave.
Cheyenne, WY 82002
(307) 777-7690
http://www.k12.wy.us/

Wyoming Parent Education Network
500 W. Lott St., Ste. A
Buffalo, WY 82834
(307) 684-7441
http://www.wpen.net/

Books

Clark, Sondra. *77 Creative Ways Kids Can Serve*. Indianapolis: Wesleyan Publishing House, 2008.

Erlbach, Arlene. *The Kids' Volunteering Book*. Minneapolis, MN: Lerner Publications, 2003.

Gay, Kathleen. *Volunteering: The Ultimate Teen Guide*. Lanham, MD: The Scarecrow Press, 2007.

Lewis, Barbara. *The Kid's Guide to Service Projects: Over 500 Service Ideas for Young People Who Want to Make a Difference*. Minneapolis: Free Spirit Publishing, 2009.

Rusch, Elizabeth. *Generation Fix: Young Ideas for a Better World*. Hillsboro, OR: Beyond Words Publishing, Inc., 2002.

Works Consulted

AmeriChild. "The Cost of Child Poverty in America." http://americhild.org/

Builder's Club of American Canyon Middle School. http://www3.nvusd.k12.ca.us/education/components/scrapbook/default.php?sectiondetailid=18467&&PHPSESSID=ea3fccbd122e00939861825c09e46b5c.

Campbell, Jeffrey and Alan Bigger. "Cleanliness and Learning in Higher Education." *Facilities Manager*, July/August 2008.

Centers for Disease Control. "School Health Policies and Programs Study." 2006. http://www.cdc.gov/HealthyYouth/shpps/2006/factsheets/pdf/FS_Overview_SHPPS2006.pdf

Corporation for National and Community Service. "Community Service and Service Learning in America's Schools." 2008. http://www.nationalservice.gov/pdf/08_1112_lsa_prevalence_factsheet.pdf

Debruin, Isral. "City's Schools Raise More than $11K to Help Haitians." *Wauwatosa Now*, March 3, 2010. http://www.wauwatosanow.com/news/86265757.html

Friedman, Jenny. *The Busy Family's Guide to Volunteering*. Beltsville, MD: Robins Lane Press, 2003.

Garton, Christie. "Ways to Help the 49 Million Americans and Children Going Hungry This Year." *USA Today*, November 18, 2009.

HandsOn Network. "Reduce the Drop-out Rate by Leveraging the Power of Service in Every School." http://handsonnetwork.org/impact/education

Hansen, Barbara J., and Philip English Mackey. *Your Public Schools: What You Can Do to Help Them*. North Haven, CT: Catbird Press, 1993.

Isaac Dickson Hot Chocolate 10K and Kids Hill Climb. http://www.hotchocolate10k.com/Default.aspx

"News." *Scholastic Junior,* March 30, 2009.

The Pew Center on the States. "One in 100: Behind Bars in America 2008." February 28, 2008, p .15. http://www.pewcenteronthestates.org/uploadedFiles/One%20in%20100.pdf

St. Charles County Division of Environmental Services. "Recycling Facts." http://www.scchealth.org/docs/es/docs/recycle/recycling_facts.html

Schoop, Kini. "56 Years Later and Still Unique: Trick-or-Treat for UNICEF." *UNICEF Press Centre*, 2006. http://www.unicef.org/media/media_36407.html.

Sims, Sandra. "How to Organize a 5K Run/Walk." *Step By Step Fundraising*. http://stepbystepfundraising.com/how-to-organize-a-5k-run-walk/

"Skyline Students Raise $400 to Help Beautify School." *[Wilmington, Delaware] News Journal,* February 7, 2010.

Sweet, Lynn. "Michelle Obama Pitches Governors on Her Childhood Obesity Plan." *Chicago Sun-Times,* February 22, 2010. http://blogs.suntimes.com/sweet/2010/02/michelle_obama_pitches_governo.html

Treadway, Tyler. "11-year-old's Idea Grows into Backpack Drive 'Kids Helping Others.'" *TCPalm.com,* February 2, 2010. http://www.tcpalm.com/news/2010/feb/02/11-year-olds-idea-grows-into-backpack-drive-kids/

U.S. Environmental Protection Agency. "Non-Hazardous Waste." http://www.epa.gov/osw/nonhaz/index.htm

U.S. General Accounting Office. "School Facilities: Condition of America's Schools." GAO/HEHS-95-61. Washington, DC: GAO, 1995. http://www.gao.gov/archive/1995/he95061.pdf

On the Internet

Get Kids in Action. "Exercise for Kids." http://www.getkidsinaction.org/exercise/

Rebuild America's Schools. "Schools in Need." http://www.rebuildamericasschools.org/Need.html

Run Walk Ride Foundation. "RWRF 101." http://runwalkride.com/marketing_101.asp

Index

Claire O'Neal has written over a dozen books for Mitchell Lane Publishers, including *Ways to Help in Your Community* in this series. She holds degrees in English and Biology from Indiana University, and a Ph.D. in Chemistry from the University of Washington. Claire enjoys volunteering at her church and in community clean-up efforts. She lives in Delaware with her husband and two young boys, and serves as PTA vice president at her sons' elementary school.